What Readers Thought Of The Book

"It is a step-by-step guide on how to set up and run an effective in-house marketing program." — David Moskowicz, VP of Plama, LLP

"An enjoyable read. Written by an author that has been there and done that." — George Porter, VP Business Development

"I like when a point is made he then presents real life examples." — Dennis Pearsall, General Contractor

"It has changed the way we look at marketing and sales." — Nick Costellano, President of Castle Corporation

"It is a light and easy read, but gets down to basics of how a marketing program should be setup and run." — Frank Tagliaferi, Civil Engineer

BEST LITTLE MARKETING BOOK EVER

Nothing Happens Till...
Somebody
Sells Something

Fred Coldwell

authorHOUSE®

AuthorHouse™
1663 Liberty Drive
Bloomington, IN 47403
www.authorhouse.com
Phone: 1-800-839-8640

First published by AuthorHouse 1/19/2010

ISBN: 978-1-4490-5637-7 (e)
ISBN: 978-1-4490-5636-0 (sc)
ISBN: 978-1-4490-5635-3 (hc)

Library of Congress Control Number: 2009912793

Printed in the United States of America
Bloomington, Indiana

This book is printed on acid-free paper.

Introduction

To everyone who reads this book and takes something away that they can use to better their professional career, you and I have Mr. Joseph Christman publisher of the Mid-Atlantic Real Estate Journal, to thank. For without his friendship and encouragement this book would have never happened. And to Lea Christman, for without her graphic eye and creative input there is no telling what this book would have looked like.

Thank you, Joe and Lea.

This book was written for the new business development/sales professional as a step-by-step "how to" approach to help you succeed. For the seasoned professional, who sometimes misplaces the basics and needs to get back on track, use this as a back to basics refresher.

What's Inside

Chapter One
"What Goes Wrong"
"You Got The Job…"

*"I love this part, you arrive for your first day on the job,
you meet everyone in the office, then your new Boss says
"…congratulations – now go out and sell something…"*

The other day I was talking to the owner of a medium size construction company, who has gone through not ONE or TWO but THREE Business Development people in one year. Let's call him JOHN – because that is his name – John, hope you are reading this. John even let me interview the third one 30 days before he fired her and she was good. John owns and operates a really good, midsize construction company; he wanted to grow his business, but now feels there is no Business Development person out there who can help. John is a real "hands on" type of guy and therein lies part of the problem.

Like some of you, I have been around "THE HORN" (whatever that means) more than once and feel I know my profession. As do many small and medium size business owners feel they know theirs. Most have gotten to where they are through hard work and one or two loyal clients. They know the loss of any one of those clients could mean the end of their firm, as they know it. Also most (if not all) want to grow their business. As their business grows they reach a point where they realize that they are "wound tight in first gear." They begin to realize that if they are out building their business they are not around to run their business. They cannot do it ALL. So they hire someone to do the part they understand the least.

That is when the Business Development "Professional" arrives on the scene. You answer the company

ad for a Business Development professional, you interview and, low and behold, the job is yours. You are the
"NEW" Business Development person for XYZ Company.

---

*"I love this part, you arrive for your first day on the job,
you meet everyone in the office, then your new
Boss says "...congratulations – now go out
and sell something..." or something like it.*

Well when the sale of a lifetime does not happen within the first week or two. He starts to won-
der if YOU were the right decision and soon thereaf-
ter you are then told how you should be doing your job.

You would not think of telling him
how to build a building. Here is how it begins:

• I want you to stay in the office and do telemarketing.

- I want you out of the office and doing cold calls.

- I want you to do direct mail.

- I want you to design brochures.

- Etc., etc., etc.

When the results are still less than expected, frustration and disappointment set in. He feels YOUR approach was flawed, YOU did not execute "THE PLAN" properly (if there even was a plan), YOU did not work hard enough, or YOU do not know what you are doing, along with enough blame and guilt to sink a ship or at least sink into clinical depression.

At this point I must set the record straight or at least my interpretation of it. SALES are when you go out and get the customers to buy something. MARKETING is when you get the customers to want to buy it and the most successful approach of all in acquiring new business is a combination of both. This is not to say you have to hire two people, but understand there is a difference. Both disciplines support each other.

Also, developing a new client does not happen in a day, a week, a month or sometimes even years. Remember that new client does not know you or your company, and unless you give them a reason to, they could not be bothered. They most likely have someone providing what you have to offer (although yours is better) and to make matters worse they are called on every day by your competition. But do not fear most of your competition fails to distinguish themselves also.

It is said that when soliciting a new client who has never heard of you, they must hear of you and/or see you at least seven times before they will even consider setting up an appointment with you to hear what you have to say. Just like building a building, Business Development takes time and is a multi-disciplinary profession. Our tools are many and varied and are all directed to that moment when, after you have made your presentation, that new client requests your proposal and/or signs on the dotted line. But we are getting ahead of ourselves. In the next several chapters I will be discussing the tools you need and how to use them to be successful. These tools include developing a database, database management, direct mail, literature, company brochures, cold calls, warm calls, new client presentations, trade shows, marketing in poor economic conditions, and attitude and persistence, etc. Hope you enjoy.

"SALES are when you get the customers to buy something. MARKETING is when you get the customer to want to buy it and the most successful approach of all in acquiring new business is a combination of both."

Chapter Two
"Who You Gonna Call..."
Your Database

"It has WORTH and should be protected."

In our first chapter we discussed how you got your new job and what can go wrong. But now that you have it, it is your responsibility to find that ever-elusive new business for which you were hired. Now who do you contact to get it? Are we talking about a list of potential clients? Yes and No. We are talking about a real live sort-able, search-able, delete-able, add-able, functional database.

Now you may ask, "Where does one start?" I would start with the names and addresses of those you are currently doing business with; their company name, contact person, address, phone number, the type of projects they are doing, and any future work that may be on the horizon. A word to the wise "it is easier to keep an existing client than to find and romance a new one." More often than not these customers are overlooked in the daily rush to find new ones.

First of all, remember that a database of existing and potential clients is and always will be "A Work in Progress." It is never finished; it is constantly being added to, adjusted and deleted from. Also once established it is considered a corporate asset. It has WORTH and should be protected.

Also once established it is considered a corporate asset. It has WORTH and should be protected.

It may not be obvious but there is an endless source of new contacts that flow through your office everyday. The following is a list of new contact sources that continue to work well for me.

FIRST – Trade Journals, Trade Newspapers, Trade Magazines, Trade Shows, etc... are excellent sources. You as the Business Development person, should review them whenever they become available. There you will find companies which you may never have heard of, many with the name of a contact person, address and phone numbers, but almost always the article will state what those companies are doing and where. Now you may be too late for the project mentioned in the article, but these people always have the next project in mind and you are right on time for that one.

SECOND – Almost every publication publishes an annual list of names for the TOP whatever, 50, 100, and 150 and so on in various fields. Review these lists and add to your database those of interest. For me the Mid-Atlantic Real Estate Journal has been an excellent contact source.

THIRD - "Selective" tradeshows. Some say they are a waste of time. Let it be known, that if you pick the right shows they can be a "GOLD MINE." We exhibit at only three shows a year and every year we walk away with at least one or two new clients/projects per show. Remember to Collect Business Cards. These are real live, eating, drinking people with heartbeats, not vacant lots and tombstones. Add them to your database.

FOURTH - Chambers of Commerce and Economic Development Councils are excellent sources for leads and personal contacts. I have gotten some of my biggest leads from casual conversations with chamber members.

Using all the above should give you a quality start for new contacts in your database. But what information should you be collecting? My current database is small with 1,876 contacts. I track names (first and last), titles, ad-

dress, phone numbers, zip codes, e-mail addresses, web-
sites, secretary names, type of businesses, where I got
them as a contact, date, time and subject of our last conversation, date and description of my last mailing to them,
date and time and details of any conversations, meetings,
etc., etc. Reason, I don't know about you but I have a hard
time remembering lunch let alone what I said to someone
I hardly know three weeks, four days and six hours ago.

Does this sound like a logistical nightmare? Have no
fear; there are several programs out there to help you handle
all this information. I prefer Symantec's ACT. I have it on
my laptop and after every client contact I record what was
said, to whom, what literature I left and so on. Now I am not
promoting ACT. It just happens to be the one I use. There are
several programs available. Find the one that best suites you.

Now you may ask, why go through all this trouble?

Well as they say, "The devil is in the details." Here is an example as to why. The "GATEKEEPER" (and we all know who she is) the one whose job it is to keep you, the Business Development/Sales person, away from her Boss, gets your call. You ask for her Boss. She asks, "What is this in reference to?" (NEVER be anything but truthful here. It will come back to haunt you). You tell her and she says if he is interested he will call you, Good Bye. Click. "That was quick." Lions 1 - Christians Nothing...

Here is another approach and this did happen. Now I made a cold call and dropped off some literature (the development of such we will discuss in the next chapter). As I walked into their offices, the receptionist/gatekeeper was talking to another employee about her brother being very sick. As I dropped off our literature I made it a point to get her name. I followed up with a phone call the next day and said, "Hello Mary, this is Fred from XYZ Design Company. I was in your office the other day and you were talking about your brother being sick, is he OK?" I was genuinely concerned and we discussed his illness. As it turned out, a member of my family had the same illness several years ago. The gate-keeper turned out to be very nice and ended up assisting me in getting an appointment with her Boss. Believe me, without my notes, and in the turmoil of everyday business I may not have remembered about her brother, the presentation would not have been made and the sale would never have happened.

It is the personal relationships you develop that will make things happen. Otherwise you are just a stranger on the street and your mom always told you not to talk to strang-ers. As a Business Development person I make hundreds of calls and from time to time get calls from people that I bare-ly remember calling. When the phone rings, our reception-ist asks for the person's name and company. She then tells me who is on the phone and the company they represent. I type the name and/or company into the database and within seconds I know what our last conversation was about, what literature I have sent them, and what projects they have coming up. It makes the caller feel like I remembered them and their company. I like it because it makes me seem intelligent and on top of my game. When in reality I am just crafty.

"It is the personal relationships you develop that will make things happen. Otherwise you are just a stranger on the street and your mom always told you not to talk to strangers."

Also BACKUP your database frequently - at least once a week. For without it you are dead in the water. If something ever happened to mine I would hang myself in the men's room with my pantyhose.

Chapter Three
"Don't leave all your candy in the lobby..."
Company Literature

"With a superior look on his face, I then asked with a confident smile, "and what do you use for follow up?"

All right you are the new Business Development person, and you have a good handle on your client database. Now what's next? Your company's literature. "You can't leave home with out it..." Like one set of construction drawings cannot be used to build every building, no one piece of literature can be used for every occasion. I divide my literature into four categories

(1) Literature I hand out during cold calls and warm calls

(2) Literature I mail

(3) Corporate literature

(4) "Special Stuff"

First let's talk about literature that you hand out while making cold calls. I was having lunch with a good friend of mine who is also in business development for a large construction company. We were discussing the hand out materials we each use when calling on potential clients. Both being very competitive, the conversation turned into "I'll show you mine if you show me yours." After a few guarded moments he produced a two-inch thick binder filled with professionally taken color photographs and descriptions of every project the company has ever done. It was impressive and on a per unit basis it must cost a fortune and he hands them out on routine sales calls. Now it was my turn. I pulled out a (one) 4 x 6 inch color postcard with a skeleton laying over an architectural drawing board with the caption "Have your heard from your architect lately," Cost per unit around two cents.

"Have you heard from your architect lately"

With a superior look on his face, I then asked with a confident smile, "and what do you use for follow up?"

The look from superiority to "I've just been had" took less then a second. I asked, "What do you do for follow-up?"- He replied, "a phone call, and you?" I then showed him my next jewel, a skeleton sitting at an architectural drawing board with the caption, "There is no fat in our proposals."

And they just keep coming - all seven of a skeleton card series. Each card addressed a developer's complaint when working with architects. Then 28 additional 4 x 6 inch cards, one for each project we designed. It is my opinion he left all his candy in the lobby and had nothing new to show the potential client on subsequent calls or during a client presentation. I have every project on a 4 x 6 inch post card with my business card attached. I leave a different card every time I call on a potential client. I can call on a potential client 34 times and show them something new each time. Remember to keep track of everything you leave with a client in the database; you don't want to show them the same thing twice unless they ask for it. Each image is loaded on my office computer and I print them out as I need them on a color desktop printer. There are no large printing costs and no inventory of literature that may never be used. And I can customize each piece when necessary, like adding what awards that project won, etc. My appointment rate is a little better then his but my cost per appointment is a lot less.

Mailed literature is pretty straightforward. Mailed literature is usually a result of some sort of client contact; a phone conversation, casual meeting or as an introductory piece when you know something about the client. It includes a cover letter outlining what we discussed and/or a qualifying statement like "I have enclosed a sampling of the type of buildings we discussed." Again don't give them everything.

Follow up with a phone call within the week (which you entered in your data base to do that day) and ask for an appointment to go over your additional portfolio. Make sure you enter into your database a copy of the letter and a list of exactly what you sent them. When you get that appointment it is now time for the big guns – your corporate literature.

Corporate literature is where you let it all hang out. This literature is used during presentations to potential clients. It should represent your very best work not only in your services or products but also in your presentation technique.

Do not include photographs of products or services that the client has no interest in. This may sound obvious, but resist the urge to present your entire menu when he only wants soup. If a potential client is into widgets don't show him whatnots or whatevers. It will only dilute your credibility as an expert in his field of interest. However, you may want to consider including ancillary items that are compatible with and/or enhance your product or service.

Your literature can be in high quality 8 ½ x 11 inch binders, 24 x 36 inch mounted, laminated and edged photographs, a Power Point presentation, whatever. But, whatever format you select, it has to be **your very best.**

Now I seldom leave any literature behind after the presentation. This is something you may consider doing. But when I return to the office, I send or hand deliver a thank you letter for the meeting, review what was discussed and include materials on those specific items the client expressed an interest in. This gives me another chance for a "face to face."

Remember just because you made your presentation, client contact after the presentation is crucial. After the presentation, schedule follow up activities in your database so you will not forget. Now for the "Special or Fun Stuff." This is what you develop when you really want to get someone's attention or, after all your efforts, nothing seems to have worked.

An Example: I found out that a potential client (one I have been calling on) was having trouble with his current architect who was not returning his calls in a timely fashion. Our office has a color plotter. I used the plotter with photographic paper and printed out a 24 x 36 inch poster of our Skeleton lying over a drawing board with the caption "Have You Heard From Your Architect Lately?" and our name and logo. I rolled it in a tube and overnighted it to the potential client. Then followed up the next afternoon with a phone call. Almost every time I get their attention and the chance to talk to the person I wanted to talk to.

Another Example: I have called on this company for

over a year. If I was told once, I was told a 100 times that Mr.

Jones would call me back. Out of frustration I plotted out a 24 x

36 inch poster of our Skeleton sitting at a desk with one hand on

the phone and the other with a pencil on an appointment book

with the caption "Still Waiting For Your Call" and our name.

Still Waiting For Your Call ...

I have still not gotten the account, but

when we see each other at a function we laugh

and say hello. That's more than I had before.

When developing your literature remember - way too

many companies are pushing what they have to sell without taking the time to understand what the client needs. Your literature should address client needs and how your products or services can satisfy that need.

Example: If you work for a construction company, or even a manufacturer, along with the type of construction or product you produce, you can address value engineering, on time product delivery, your ability to be on or under budget, your ability to problem solve, etc. and do it in an interesting way.

Think ouside of the box – Don't be afraid to try something different. Have fun with it...

Chapter Four
"The Good, The Bad, and The Ugly"
Sales Calls

It was the first time in my professional career that I entered a building, left, was called back, to be thrown out.

A quick review, you found and got the job as a Business Development/Sales professional, your database is well under way, your literature is in order, and now it is time to do your mailings and cold calls.

You are well on your way to addressing the issue that a new client (one that has never heard of you or your company before) needs to hear from you or see you at least seven times before they will entertain the idea of a face-to-face presentation of your products/services.

Let's start with your mailings, keep them small.

Mail only enough that you can personally follow up on (drive to or call) within a week. After that it is mostly forgotten. Remember you absolutely, positively must document what you mailed and to whom in your database along with the date you are going to follow up.

Blanket mailing of several hundred or even thousands at one time (unless you are consumer marketing, which is based on volume) is mostly a waste of money. If you insist on going the mass mailing route remember this: on an average expect a response rate of one quarter of one percent. So if you mail out 1,000 brochures expect 2.5 inquiries. If you close one in four sales calls (a high rate) you should mail out around 2,000 brochures to get 4 appointments to make one sale. A mailing like this, once a month for a year will cost you around $10,560 (at 44 cents a unit) in postage alone and if your brochures cost $1.00 each to print you just sent $34,560 of your hard earned money to a landfill.

A friend of mine, JOHN, - remember him from the first chapter? – INSTRUCTED his Business Development person to mail out 300 brochures. When he got no response he let his Business Development person go. Wrong move all around, you are selling professional services and/or products through relationships, which you are trying to develop. Your unsolicited mass mailing of brochures, with no follow up, I am sorry to say, is "junk mail." By keeping your mailings manageable, and very targeted you keep your costs to a minimum and, with follow up, will get a greater response for your marketing dollar.

I would love to tell the story of the world's greatest direct mail piece that produced a 50 percent response, while violating all the established rules, but we will leave that for another time.

Now it is time for your follow up. Of those you mailed

your literature to, (if possible) drive to their office, walk in, and hand out another piece of literature with business card attached to the receptionist. Tell her to tell Mr. Jones (your contact) that you would like to call for an appointment. Don't even mention your mailing and don't ask to see him. Remember you're uninvited, he won't have time for you now and he won't in the future without an appointment. When your contact receives your mailing and you follow up within the same week you have made an impression. Either that day or no later than the following day, follow up with a phone call and ask for an appointment. Don't get your hopes up, it may take several more of these mailings and visits to gain your new client's confidence and make them aware that you are here to stay.

Another benefit in going to the client's office is that you get a chance to qualify them as a potential client. A HUGE word of caution here, I was calling on a builder to drop off a marketing piece. As I drove up, I noticed that his office was in a run down ranch house with two beat up pickup trucks outside. In my infinite wisdom I qualified him as unworthy. Six months later I was driving down a road three miles from his house and there he was building his new corporate headquarters, a modern 60,000 square foot office building with six new trucks outside. I am still beating my head against the dashboard every time I drive by.

That was a bad time. There have been really good times also. I was going to drop off a marketing piece when, entering the lobby, the person I wanted to see was standing right there. That presented an excellent opportunity to do a 60 second overview of our firm and to ask for an appointment. I was told to contact his secretary and an appointment was set up a week later. Came to find out he used that time to check out our web site and asked around about our firm before he committed himself. A public forum like a lobby is not the place for the hard sell.

At times I have been asked by a secretary to send in all my literature and he will review it later. Don't do it. If you do you will have nothing new to present as a follow up. Send him selected pieces every other week, a subtle reminder that you're still there ready to do business.

So we have covered the Good and the Bad of client visits. Now for the Ugly. This one has to be a classic. I was calling on a homebuilder in New Jersey who will remain nameless. Those of you who know him or someone like him will recognize his style.

I was doing my follow up after a mailing and pulled into a parking space outside of Anonymous Home Builders. With literature in hand, I walked in and approached the receptionist, handed her the literature and asked if she would tell Mr. Nameless that I would like to call to set up an appointment. She said she would and I left the building.

While getting into my car, she came running up to me and said that Mr. Nameless would like to see me NOW. Could not believe my luck. With a grin that was only hampered by my ears, I gladly got out of the car and followed her back into the building. Thoughts like What Timing, Major Project Ahead, and He Has a Problem and Needs Our Help just kept coming. We entered the building and walked to his office. The door was open and I could see there was a meeting going on inside so I waited outside the door. He called for me to come in. Feeling uneasy I said, "Mr. Nameless, I will be happy to wait." His response, "NO, get in here and what do you want?"

All eyes were on the stranger in the doorway. I entered, mentioned where I was from and said I would like to set up an appointment to see him. He responded with a Booming "Why?" I thought it was quite obvious, I represent a design company, what do you think I want to talk to you about, "the weather?" Undaunted and smiling I presented my best 60-second company overview and again asked for an appointment at a more opportune time. He bellowed from across the room "Get Out - Not Interested."

It was the first time in my professional career that I entered a building, left, was called back, to be thrown out.

I came to find out that Hank is that way with everyone. I guess that if the job was easy everybody would want to do it.

... a new client (one that has never heard of you or your company before) needs to hear from you or see you at least seven times before they will entertain the idea of a face-to-face presentation of your products/services.

Chapter Five
"Make My Decision Easy ..."
Sales Presentations

It was like showing a customer the space shuttle when he only wanted a Piper Cub. He listened intently, and then, after the presentation, went to look for a Piper Cub dealer.

As a quick review, you have been hired as the company's new Business Development/Sales professional, your database is up and running, your literature is great, you did your mailings and low, and behold, a potentially new client wants to talk to you and an appointment is ready to be scheduled. This is what you have been working for, your day to show what you've got. Well maybe not you, "Your Boss."

Now most Business Development people work toward scheduling client appointments not necessarily for themselves but for themselves and their Boss who wants to be involved in meeting the client for the first time and making the presentation.

Usually the meeting is in the client's office. However if the opportunity presents itself, invite them to your office and introduce them to your staff. It will make them feel welcome, important, and comfortable knowing the people in your organization. No matter where the meeting is held it is YOUR responsibility to - Be Prepared - not your boss.

When setting up a time and place for the presentation tell the client that you have an "extensive portfolio" and to make the meeting as "productive as possible" ask what type of project/product is he looking for. He may say that he does not have anything specific in mind at this time, but believe me he has something in mind or you would not be there. Remember our chapter on literature? Well this is the time you bring your very best portfolio. It can be 24 x 36 inch color photography, mounted, and laminated with edges, a Power Point presentation or just a high quality binder. But whatever you bring it has to be your best.

Be on time, not 30 minutes early and for sure not 30 minutes late. Five minutes early is perfect. If you have to stay in the car or get a cup of coffee, do it. If you are going to be late, call the client. Most of the time it may not be a problem but if you don't call and just show up late it leaves a bad impression and that is not the way you want to start out.

Most of the time, once you arrive, you will be escorted into a conference room and will have a moment or two before your client and possibly his staff arrive to hear what you have to say. This is your time to take control, make the room yours. If necessary re-arrange the room – setup any displays, products and/or photographs you brought along, select your seating (with you facing the door and their backs to the door you're less likely to be casually interrupted).

I remember a time once when a boss of mine and I were making a presentation to a developer. The developer was looking for an Age Restricted Community. The developer already had a basic site plan and if we were going to get the job we had to come up with something better. Several weeks earlier I did some research as to how we could do better and came up with the idea of an Age Qualified Neighborhood, with walking trails and benches through the open space, ponds, a walk - to retail center with an ice cream parlor, dry cleaners, pharmacy, etc., with a gated community look and feel. Presented the idea to my boss and he liked the idea so a new site plan with elevations with this new approach was developed.

Once we arrived and sat down, my boss opened the presentation and was doing fine, until he mentioned that I had done some research to come up with this new plan. I thought that was my cue so I expounded on why we thought this new approach would set his community apart. Let's just say it was the wrong move. After the meeting and even before we reached the lobby he let me know in no uncertain terms that he makes the presentations.

So, assuming this is your first presentation with your boss. Lay out the groundwork ahead of time. A day before the meeting or no later than the drive to the meeting bring your boss up to date on the contacts you have had with the client and what got you to this meeting. Casually mention that you would like to start out the meeting since you have been in contact with the client and then you will turn the presentation over to him or her. Once the meeting is coming to an end you can close the meeting by asking for the job/project/sale.

Many a good presentation goes unrewarded because no one asked for the job or sale. Also remember this. Show them what they want to see. Show them what they are interested in.

It only reinforces your position as an expert in what they are looking for. If you are a supplier and the builder is looking for low-end materials to keep the cost down, don't show him your high end line. You will blow yourself out of the water. That is unless you can sell it at your competitor's low-end price.

I remember a presentation when the client was looking for a mid-rise apartment complex. The presentation however was an aerial view of an urban re-development plan, which had a smattering of mid-rise apartments between the high-rise office buildings, river walk, stadium, government buildings, theaters, etc. It was like showing a customer the space shuttle when he only wanted a Piper Cub. He listened intently, and then, after the presentation, went to look for a Piper Cub dealer.

It was like showing a customer the space shuttle when he only wanted a Piper Cub. He listened intently, and then, after the presentation, went to look for a Piper Cub dealer.

The client wants to work with someone with the expertise that they need no matter how simple the project. Present yourself as that expert.

Now I know you have a lot more to offer and that you want the client to understand your full capabilities. So at the end of the meeting suggest, that if he has time, he visit your website for a more complete understanding of your firm's products and services.

By setting up a time and place for you to make a presentation, your potential client is asking you for help – he is asking you to make his decision for him.

He does not want to interview 10 suppliers. He wants you to convince him that you are the one. He is asking for you to "Make My Decision Easy" to select you.

HE IS ASKING YOU TO MAKE HIS DECISION EASY.

...if you have a choice between his place or yours choose yours, be on-time, be prepared, show him what HE wants to see and ask for the job.

Chapter Six
*"It Is Not What You Pay Them -
It Is What You Don't Pay Them"*
Compensation

McDonalds probably retains its people better.

Ok, so far you got the job, your database is going great, your literature is working, your presentations are dynamic. What about compensation?

The other day I was talking to a friend of mine. He had just left a Business Development position with a large construction company. As we were talking, the subject of "turnover" in the Business Development/sales profession came up. He had conducted a VERY informal survey in which he looked at 25 firms that had a Business Development person in place. Three years later only three firms had the same Business Development person in place.

41

McDonalds   probably   retains   it's   people   better.

As   a   result,   this   chapter   on   compensation   and   Business   Development   was   born.

We are going to briefly discuss some of the various forms of compensation and their pitfalls as I see it.
Usually compensation takes one of three forms: all salary, salary plus bonus/commission or straight commission.
I guess how you look at compensation depends on which
side of the table you are sitting on. The owner of the company wants to maximize profit, the Business Development person wants to be rewarded for his or her efforts. It
should also be taken into consideration that to do the job
right Business Development is not a nine to five job. There
are evening meetings with Chambers of Commerce, trade
shows, industry meetings and a lot of cold calling and follow ups that do not fit within the nine to five envelope.

First let's talk about straight salary. A lot of companies hire people who are young, inexperienced with no or little product knowledge at a low salary. They are told to go out and sell or at least setup appointments for the owner so they can go sell the prospect. This truly is a "you get what you pay for" form of compensation and is the basis for the large turnover in our industry. If the salary is low, unfortunately, so will be the effort and experience level. However, the successful companies have elected to take another approach. Pay a good salary to someone who knows the industry or has the right attitude (a subject we will be discussing in chapter IX), has the contacts or at least can talk the language to get in the door. This approach can only provide the company dividends within the industry as a stable firm to do business with. It just makes sense.

What about the straight commission approach? In several industries the long lead-time from initial client contact to finished project and final payment may and does take years. Along the way a lot of things can and do go wrong, which your firm has no control over. Like the client applying for and not receiving zoning changes, project financing or land purchases falling through, under bidding of competing companies, even your own proposal being too high.

Although some people may thrive on a straight commission policy, most cannot survive. The advantage to the company is that there is little or no expense until the project is complete. Should you go this route as a Business Development professional be sure the commission level is high enough to cover those projects that never see the light of day and that your agreement is written down and ironclad. I know it is not romantic when you are on the "new job honeymoon", but the honeymoon will end.

As an example, I had heard through the grapevine

that this company was considering developing a mixed-use medical facility. They owned the land and their plans were to develop an age-restricted community, with an assisted care facility and a medical center - really nice project. I called on this client for over two years and made several presentations at various executive levels. Fees to the firm exceeded $1,000,000. When we were selected for the project the only thing that stopped my grin was my ears since my salary structure included a bonus of 10 percent of any project that brings in $500,000 or more in fees.

Work began on the site plan and phone conversations and meetings on the project were almost a daily occurrence. Until one day they just stopped. Our calls were not being answered or returned. I began to think I said something derogatory about someone's ancestry or I ran over the owner's cat and did not know it. I came to find out that another developer came along and made them an offer for the land they could not refuse and the project just went away and so did the grin. Although the firm got paid well for the work it had done, no matter how much effort was expended on my part no bonus was forth coming. So much for straight commission, but there are those who would not want to work any other way.

Then there is the salary plus bonus compensation package, most likely the best of the three options and the one that breeds the most discontentment. A base salary is established and a dollar threshold for new business beyond which the company will pay a percentage of as a bonus is established.

Take my advice work out ALL the details, get it in writing up front and have all parties sign it. A lot of companies, when they are faced with paying out a large bonus, will find all types of creative ways to either reduce the amount or eliminate it and you altogether. Here is an example. I worked for this large well-known firm that had no Business Development position until the time I went to work with them. It was a salary (although small) and bonus package that had a high dollar threshold before the bonus kicked in, but with luck I felt I could make it. Over the next six months I sold several small and medium size new accounts. But on the seventh I month sold a very large account with over 250 retail outlets in which each would be using our product. As a matter of fact every three months they would reorder. The income from this new account alone exceeded the threshold in which my bonus kicked in. Needless to say I was looking forward to a nice extra check. However at bonus time I was told "…Oh no, that bonus figure is a monthly figure not an annual one." That was my last day. Or the time when I started with a firm on a salary plus bonus package and was told that anything over $300,000 in new business fees the bonus would be 15 percent. Had a really good third year, new business fees far exceeded the $300,000 mark and at bonus time was told "…Oh, that $300,000 was only for the first year it has gone up each year since…"

This may sound like sour grapes but it is real life. There are those Business Development people who are let go because they failed to bring in the work, there are those that are let go because the firm now has enough work and it feels it does need them any more and when the work falls off they will hire another one cheaper, and there are those who leave because the company failed to live up to it's financial agreement. This is the one major cause why good Business Development people leave a company. The reality is that in the end the company really cannot afford it.

I do not mean to preach but when a company looks after its people both financially and ethically and the employees look after the company… THEY BOTH WIN.

Chapter Seven
"Where did they go...?"
Business Development/Selling In A Down Economy

*Now is the time to be that person
that "makes things happen."*

It is said that there are three types of people in this world: those who make things happen, those who watch things happen and those who ask what happened.

The other day while making client calls, I was speaking to a potential client and we were discussing the economy. He said that business was slow and that he felt one of the best ways to survive this economic crisis was to (among other things) discontinue their marketing/sales efforts until the economy improves. Being an old Navy man I thought that would be like shutting down your engines because you're in a storm. You're not really getting anywhere so why waste the money on fuel. My first thought, not the best move.

That is not to say one should not economize, cutting back hours, or shorter work weeks, etc., should the situation require it. It is said that you have to be in business to do business.

But by getting fully behind your marketing effort you will be in a better position to take advantage of what opportunities are out there and be up to speed when things do turn around.

Now is the time to be that person that "makes things happen."

There are always market segments or regions that still prosper even in an economic down - turn. There is business out there. Go and get it.

One of the best places to look is your existing customers. Relationships and price mean more now then ever before. Be sensitive to how the economic downturn has affected them and come up with creative ways that will, if they use your firm, they can save money and time. Partnering with subcontractors and venders on special programs is another great idea. They are out there looking for business also and by working together you double your chances.

We came up with and initiated a unique program that would limit clients' backend cost while at the same time covering our overhead. For the program to be successful our subcontractors had to not only agree to the idea but to become part of the process. In return they would get whatever jobs were captured by the new program. Once we explained the new program every firm agreed to participate. By partnering with our subcontractors we were able to offer a unique program, one we would never have thought of in a better economy. By including the subcontractors/venders in the process, we in effect doubled the sales efforts and established loyalties that will last for years.

Now is not the time to pull back on your marketing and sales efforts. Be creative, be aggressive, be the one that makes things happen not one of the ones that asks "what just happened?" Because, for them, the opportunities have passed them by.

But by getting fully behind your marketing effort you will be in a better position to take advantage of what opportunities are out there and be up to speed when things do turn around.

Chapter Eight
"Well Here We Are Folks…"
Trade Shows

"Do Not Expect What You Do Not Inspect."

So far the job is yours, database working, literature good, client presentations right on, compensation ok, the economy bad but we will make it.

And now trade shows. I have worked for companies that thought exhibiting at a trade show was a waste of time and money. Let me set the record straight. You pick the right shows, get a good spot, have a decent booth, and man it like you want to be there, and they can be a good source of new leads, contacts and even, low and behold, real business.

There are two types of shows; ones that your

specific target market attends and ancillary shows - they are shows where your product or service may or may not be of interest too certain attendees.

Now for picking the right show. Shows that are in your specific market are usually a good place to be and your competition thinks so too. If for no other reason it lets your current clients know that you are there and still in business. For if your not there you are out of sight and out of mind and your competition now has a chance to talk to YOUR clients. It also presents the opportunity to meet those clients with whom you may not have been able to get an appointment.

Ancillary shows are those shows that are not directly related to what you do but the people who attend these shows may have a use for your product or service. Now this is real prospecting. I remember I went to a machinery show, not because I had anything to do with machinery, but because the attendees at the show may have been in need of a new building or the renovation of an old one to house their new found machinery. Most likely your competition will not be at this type of show, because they are playing it safe and the field is all yours. Think out of the box.

Now, where are you going to put your exhibit and what it should look like? Usually, the show organizers will send you a floor plan with all the booths mapped out and numbered. So you can select your booth location(s) (they ask you for four options) on a floor plan months before a show. Try to locate your booth at the end of a row close to or on the major traffic isle or, equally as good, around the food section of the exhibit floor. Attendees like to mill around the food and you will be right there to talk to them all. Also, if the show turns out to be a dud, you don't have far to go eat your troubles away. Now these locations are premium locations and the organizers know it and will usually charge a little more for those locations.

Exhibits go from one extreme to the other. There are exhibits that pop up out of a tube and are ready in all of two minutes and there exhibits that are brought in with fork lifts and take a crew (usually a union crew) hours to set up. May I suggest something in the middle? Think about how you want to tell the world or at least the people attending the show "this is who we are." One company uses a booth made up of sections of steel tubing. When put together it looks like the structural frame work of a building. I have seen other firms use Gothic white columns made of plastic (that looked really good). Setting up usually is not too bad (unless you are late for the show, of course); it is taking it down when you are tired that ease of construction really matters. That is when you wished it came out of a tube.

I always set up my own exhibit with the help of one other person; it takes about two hours to set up and one to take down. The reason I do it! The last show I went to, I witnessed another exhibiting company that had their booth shipped to the show and arranged (so they thought) to have the show organizers set it up. On the day of the show the Business Development staff (with the president of the company in tow) showed up ten minutes before the show opened and there were their exhibit crates sitting in their booth unopened. The show was a full day the first day and half a day the second. They spent the better half of the first day setting up their booth while clients and potential clients looked on. I came to find out that when the show was over the whole business development group that was involved in the show were let go.

Remember a word to the wise

"Do Not Expect What You Do Not Inspect."

Remember something always goes wrong – PLAN FOR IT. If you think it all went smoothly, something did go wrong and you just are not aware of it yet. Now I must say most all show organizers get the job done – it is the Business Development staff that did not check and double check that are the ones in the wrong here. Don't let it happen to you. As for giveaway items, I personally   think they are a huge waste of money (sorry promotional   gimmick people) and a pain in the neck to lug around. When was the last time you attended a trade show and actually called the company whose name was on the squeegee stress reliever ball? Then at the end of the show, when all your clients have left, the vultures swoop in with bags on both arms to relieve you of your marketing dollars. Again there are exceptions to this. I was at an International Council of Shopping Centers show and the booth next to me was a manufacture of "Hot Sauce" which he gave out. It was his own product and he wanted people to try it . Good move.

Greeting trade show attendees – Now you can just sit there like a frog on a log and wait till someone comes up to you and almost no-one will. If that is the case it is going to be a very long show and a huge waste of good money.

First and foremost, when the exhibit space is open you NEVER sit down. A person representing a company sitting down with potential customers walking by is not ready to do business and business is why you are there.

You should be impeccably dressed and have a style, whatever it is. One exhibitor I know gets dressed up in a 1940 golf outfit, kickers and all, for every show. He is instantly recognizable and everybody knows him.

I am clean shaven like a NEW CUE BALL. With my black mandarin button - up shirt, black suit, socks and shoes, surrounded by the steel frame work of a building, it draws attention.

Now I do not remember everyone, as a matter of fact there are times I have to look in my wallet to remember my wife's name. But unlike my wife, these people have name tags with their names in **BIG BOLD TYPE.**

Call them by name, OUT LOUD. It will at least take them be surprise, they always smile and look to see if they know you. Ask them how they are enjoying the show. Engage them in conversation. But *NEVER, NEVER* prejudge an attendee (or anybody for that matter) by their appearance.

I was at a show when an older man walked by in faded jeans and a jean shirt with unkept hair pulled back in a ponytail and loafers. I had an appointment with him several weeks before and recognized him at once. He looked the same at this show as he had during our presentation. He was president of one of the largest companies I have ever called on. With out a doubt he was worth hundreds of millions. We recognized each other and had a really nice conversation. As he walked away, I saw the other exhibitors ignore him and some were almost rude. I thought, what a mistake.

NEVER take anyone for granted by the way they look. You pass some of the most influential people every day and never know it. Without knowing it they may very well be that one client you always wanted. Pick a good show, have a nice exhibit, don't sit down, greet everyone the same way, have fun and business will come your way.

"If you sit down you are not ready to do business." If *you take nothing else from this chapter this should be it.*

Chapter Nine
"If It Was Easy
Everybody Would Be Doing It…"
PERSISTENCE & ATTITUDE

*If it wasn't for persistence and having
the right attitude, I would have given
up long ago and never gotten through the door.*

These two go hand in hand PERSISTENCE & AT-TITUDE. In the face of constant rejection it is important to keep going and to maintain a "Can Do" positive attitude.

Now there are exceptions to almost every rule in everything you do. You call on a new client and on the very first call you sign them up. And then you call on someone for years and never get through the door. Now why would anyone in their right mind keep doing this? Because you have researched that company and know that they are the type of client your company wants and needs.

There was such a company in our operating area. They were successful, paid all their bills on time and were loyal to their venders. The type of company every one wants to do business with. I called on them every other month for over four years. They got to know me and I got to know them. But still no work until one day the phone rang, it was the president of that company saying he may have missed the boat and wanted to know if we could help. They were building a large project and were using the same venders they always did. Unfortunately, or fortunately for me, that vender lacked the expertise in this product type and the product was not selling. Years of persistence paid off. The project was redesigned and is now back on track and we are now the flavor of the month. It took over four years for this client to even consider us but he knew we were always there ready to do business with him. Was it worth it? Absolutely.

Remember the one constant in the world is change.

If it wasn't for persistence and having the right attitude I would have given up long ago and never gotten through the door.

There is a quote by Calvin Coolidge, that best sums up the persistence part pretty well. It goes: "Nothing in the world can take the place of persistence. Talent will not; nothing is more common than unsuccessful people with talent. Genius will not; unrewarded genius is almost a proverb. Education will not; the world is full of educated derelicts. Persistence and determination alone are omnipotent."

The power of Persistence is true as far as it goes. But attitude is equally important. "Nothing can stop a man with the right mental attitude from achieving his goal; nothing on earth can help a man with the wrong mental attitude," Thomas Jefferson.

If you combine persistence and the right attitude the world is your limit.

Several years ago, well decades really, I was out of work and looking for a new job. I would get up every morning get dressed as if I was going to work, sit down at my computer and send out resumes and cover letters. Two days later, I would make my follow up phone calls. During one call I was speaking to the receptionist and she mentioned that they could not find my resume and asked if I would send them another. I said that I was in the area (not really, I was over an hour away) and would be glad to drop one off. She said, "No need just send one in." Remember she is "Mary The Gatekeeper" and her job, as we now know, Keep You Away From Her Boss. I said it was really not a problem at all.

I drove to their office, walked in and said, "Good morning. My name is Fred and I spoke to you earlier this morning. I am here to drop off another copy of my resume." She accepted it with a smile. Then I said, "Since I am here would you check to see if Mr. Jones has a moment to see me?" She didn't quite snarl but it was close. Reluctantly, she got up and disappeared around the corner. A moment later she came back and I thought I saw a small frown on her face as she said Mr. Jones would see me.

She escorted me back to his office; I walked in and waited to be invited to sit down. He opened the conversation by pointing to the pile of resumes on his desk which was over eight inches high and said, "I found your resume here in this pile," It was the perfect opportunity.

I said, "Am I glad I stopped in here today. I just saved

you from weeks worth of work." He looked puzzled. I continued, "It would have taken you weeks to read through all those resumes, select those you wanted to interview, schedule the initial interviews and then schedule a second round of interviews just to end up with me in the end anyway. I am really happy that I stopped in this morning." He looked dumbfounded. Then smiled and said, "The job is yours." I was no more or less qualified then the other candidates who sent in a resume. I was just a little more persistent with the right attitude. Remember, if you cannot sell yourself and the company you represent with enthusiasm every time find another line of work.

There was a story I heard about a corporate pilot and his rather unusual job interview. He responded to an ad for a corporate pilot for the chief executive of a large corporation. The ad listed the qualifications and requirements for the job. When he arrived for his 9 a.m. interview he saw 28 other corporate pilots there also waiting to be interviewed. All had appointments scheduled for 9 a.m. Nine o' clock came and went, then 10, 11, 12, and so on. One by one the candidates left disgruntled. At around 6 p.m. that evening the room was down to two candidates and the other candidate finally left. He was the only one left in the room. A few moments later the corporate executive he was to be the pilot for came out of his office and said congratulations you got the job. It was his attitude and persistence that prevailed.

Look at it this way if you keep a positive attitude when everyone else around you is losing theirs at least you can get a chance to get on their nerves. At best you can change their attitudes around and make something positive happen.

Remember practice does not make perfect. Perfect practice makes perfect.

Remember if you cannot sell your-self and the company you represent with enthusiasm every time find another line of work.

Chapter Ten
"What Time Is It...?"
Client Communications

"How should I say this to make my point, NEVER – NEVER – NEVER..."

Let's assume for a moment that you are e-mailing someone you do not or hardly know, a prospective client for example, and this e-mail is a follow up to a cold call you made earlier that week.

How should I say this to make my point,

NEVER – NEVER – NEVER...

inject humor into your e-mails unless it is someone you know **VERY, VERY** well and you have something in common with to laugh about. To say the least it does not come across well and gives the appearance that you are not serious in your business affairs. I have read e-mails from other people who think a little humor will break the ice in an e-mail. Let's just say it seals your fate and not in a positive way. You do not know this person, you can not see their face, you do not know what kind of day they are having or even if they own a sense of humor.

Save the humor for your friends and non-business associates. It does not belong in business e-mail.

In your e-mails, phone messages and written correspondence be positive - things are going well for you and your firm - everyone wants to work with someone who is on the move and doing something positive. It is implied that you must be doing something right. It is human nature that they subconsciously hope it will rub off and that some of your luck will run their way or by associating with you they to will be more successful.

It is all in the perception. It is a lot like Regan Economics. In the early 1980s the economy was in the tank. In 1981 Ronald Regan became the 40th president of the United States. Among other things, his stimulus package was designed to tell everybody that the economy was good. He would tell anyone and everyone that would listen. He said it so often to so many people that people began to believe him and things got better.

Now I am not saying to lie, most of us are not in politics. But I am saying no customer new or old wants to associate themselves with a firm that appears to be not doing well. No matter what the reason, not doing well implies that you are not doing something right and they do not want it to rub off onto them. So keep all you communications with potential, new and existing clients positive. Your glass is more than half full and about to overflow.

There is an ethical limit to this approach, like

your company is going out of business and you are taking deposits on product that you know you can not deliver. Again this is beyond the scope of this book.

Now let's say you are trying to get an appointment
with a prospective client. In your e-mails, letters or phone
messages you are positive in your approach and outlook
– your "things are going well" message is coming through.
But how do you get their attention? How can you make your
communication stand out? One way is to be very specific as to
the time and date that you are going to call. State that you will
call, at 9:56 on Tuesday. It does not matter what time it is, it
just has to be very specific on a specific day. It can be 8:48 or
10:02 or 2:28, whatever, but make it unusual. Believe it or not
most people (if they are not in a meeting or out of the office)
will wait to see if you do what you say you are going to do.

I remember I was trying to get hold of a company

president that I believed was building a new facility. In my first e-mail I wrote that I would call him at 8:57 a.m. on Wednesday the 18th. You guessed it. At exactly 8:57 a.m. that Wednesday his phone rang. I got his secretary and was told he was not in and I asked if she would leave a message that I called. Every good secretary notes the time of a call. I told her I would call again at 10:02 on Thursday. Again I called exactly at 10:02 that Thursday and got his voice mail. Left another message on his voice mail that I would call at 3:38 next Monday. You guessed it. Exactly at 3:38 p.m. on Monday I called. This time the phone rang once and he picked it up and said, "Hello Fred, I knew it would be you."

There are several things at work here. First persistence, remember we talked about persistence and attitude in the last chapter. The other is the person I was calling (either consciously or subconsciously) wanted to see if I would do exactly what I said I would do. He did not know that I sat by the phone watching the clock for just the right moment to call. I would not let anyone talk to me, go to the bathroom, get involved in a meeting, take another call, whatever. I was not going to miss, even by a minute, my designated time to call. I was out to prove that I was the kind of person that did what they said they were going to do and, by inference, so was the firm I represented.

Now e-mails and letters are pretty straight forward. Make sure there are no spelling and grammar mistakes and that the person's name is spelled correctly, you know all the regular stuff. Again no humor, state your facts and if a follow up phone call is needed be specific about when you are going to call.

One of the hardest things to do in this job (at least for me) is to pick up the phone and make that follow up phone call. I know as many times as I do it I often make up excuses as to why this is not a good time or try to put it off for some of the stupidest reasons. But it is a necessary part of the job.

So like everything else there is a way to go about it that makes it not quite as painful. The approach is to plan the conversation out in advance, the key is to not sound like a telemarketer. Let's call it a "Conversation Chart." And I mean make a chart on paper as to what you are going to say from "Hello" to "Good By" and everything in between. Were you ever in a conversation and after it was over you say to yourself, "Oh I should have said this when they said that, it would have been a great response." Well now (in the quiet of your office or cubical whatever the case may be) is the time to plan out all those great responses and write them down in response to anticipated questions and objections. Example: You call and the secretary answers the phone. You say, "Hello, I am Bill Miller and I am with ABC Company. Is Mister Johnson in?" If the answer is "Yes" then you say "May I speak to him." If the answer is "No" then you ask "may I leave a message on his voice mail?" That is the easy stuff. But be ready just in case Mr. Johnson answers the phone. Stammering and stuttering just isn't going to work.

This is when your Conversation Chart will really pay off. When your mind slips out of gear, your Conversation Chart slips in. Example: I called and got the opportunity to speak to the president of the company unexpectedly. I mentioned that I was with an architectural firm. He stated that he has his own in-house architectural department. Was I shot down? No. I anticipated this response in my Chart and my response was, "So do several of our clients and we are able to free up their staff by doing the construction drawing for their firm enabling their staff to concentrate on the designs." Another example: I called and was told by their V.P. of construction that they already have an architectural firm and are not inter-

ested in a replacement. Again the comment was anticipated and the response, was, "I am aware of that fact. I
do not want to replace your existing firm. What I would
like is for you to consider us as an option should your
existing firm become overloaded or problems occur."

Until your responses become second nature work out your response to questions and objections in advance. Write them down, pin your chart over
the phone and you will never stammer or stutter again.

---

*Be positive in your conversations, be specific about when
you are going to call and know what you are going to say.*

Chapter Eleven
"Who me? Yes You."
Making Yourself Irreplaceable

Now everyone knows that no one is irreplaceable. If your company is closing – through no fault of your own - there is not much you can do about it. But until that time comes there are some things you can do to be sure you are one of the last to be let go. And that is to make yourself irreplaceable or at least harder than most for them to let go.

First and foremost do your job and do it to the very best of your ability. Remember it is harder to find a job than it is to work at a job.

Also **EVERYTHING** you do is noticed by someone. Now I am not a smoker and I am not picking on smok-

ers, it is that they make such an easy target. But I did no-
tice and so did the other employees and bosses in the office
that when the smokers in our office go out for their smoke
break, it took an average of 15 minutes to leave the building,
have a cigarette and then return to their desks. They usually
took two breaks a day, one in the morning and one in the
afternoon. That relates to 30 minutes a day of non-productive time that the company is paying for, in a week that is
2 ½ hours, a month 10 ¾ hours and a year 129 hours or a
little over 16 days. Everyone else in the office worked those
16 days that year. Plus the smokers got their sick days, personal days, holidays and vacation pay, like everyone else.

Now again I admit picking on the smokers is a cheap
shot but they are so obvious. Not so obvious, but at the same
time as non-productive is surfing the internet, internet shopping, personal e-mails, additions and updates to your social
networking site, playing solitaire and yes even watching

movies on your computer monitor during working hours. Now you may say that no one in their right mind would be that dumb. Someone in our office was and that person was one of the first to be let go when thing slowed down. These interferences in the work day far exceed 30 minutes a day as stated earlier and, believe it or not, they are noticed.

Monitoring of individual computer activity by management goes beyond the scope of this book. But it does happen, is happening and is on the increase. P.S. They can and do read your e-mails.

All right I admit that the above should be common sense and we are talking about making yourself irreplaceable, not doing stupid things to get yourself fired and we are talking about business development/sales.

If you are out on the road you may be out of sight but believe me you are not out of mind. I call in every morning to tell the receptionist where I am going, who I intend to see, and again every evening before she leaves the office for any messages.

If I drive by a sign of a company that could be a potential client, I call the office and tell the secretary where I am and that I just drove by XYZ company's sign and would she do a google search for me to find out who I should ask for and what type of work they do before I enter the building. You may not know it but the fact you called in from the road and asked for a google search on a potential client gets around the office and although you may be out of sight, you are out there doing your job.

During sales presentations (you know the ones you worked so hard to set up so that your boss can make the presentation) keep accurate notes as to what is being said, by whom, and who is requesting additional information.

Those notes may very well be the only documentation as to what was said during the presentation. Because after everyone leaves the table and goes back to their offices it is a matter of "who remembers what" and your notes become the definitive word. On more than one occasion, my notes have saved the day and even the smallest requests were followed up on and questions answered.

Your notes should start out with the time, date and location of the meeting and who was present. Very Important - get and give business cards to and from everyone at the outset of the meeting. You will need them for the correct spelling of their names, titles and to add anyone you do not have into your database. Now you have become more than a pretty face at these meetings, you have become a valuable asset. Once back at the office, type a condensed version of your notes into your database for future reference.

Another valuable tool is to learn additional skills that are compatible with your sales and marketing skills. These will enable you to become an even greater asset to your company and to any other company, you may be applying. But you should develop those skills on your own time. Then bring them to the office and apply them to your profession.

Example: A firm I was working for was throwing out an out-of-date computer and monitor. I rescued it and took it home. I had a very old copy of Photoshop and loaded it onto the machine and started to learn how to use the program. I would take an image of a two-story building, make it a five story, then eight story and back. I would add stone or brick to the building, grass, trees, parking lot, drive ways, clouds and skies, and so on and so on.

Then one day I took several revised elevations of the same building to the office and showed it to the partners of the firm.

Although it was the same building each revision or change made it look entirely different. I added a custom title block with the name of the building, the location and our corporate logo along the bottom. They were impressed and asked if I could do it to other buildings? "Absolutely" was the answer.

Two weeks later we presented a rendering of a proposed four-story building to a new client. The image was hand-drawn and looked like a piece of art. Although impressed, the client asked if he could see it in a two-story and six-story model. I thought my boss was going to pass out because he drew it and rendered it by hand. I got his attention and smiled and nodded my head. He instantly knew what I had in mind.

One week later we presented both the two-story and six-story models he requested. It would have taken weeks doing both over again by hand.

I had the original converted to a digital format and worked my Photoshop magic. What would have taken two to three weeks only took three to four hours. This time on company time and being paid to do it. The rest is history. I now do all image alterations for the firm, design and print all company literature as well as all advertising and promotional materials.

This supplements my business development/ sales activities and this additional skill saved the principles of the firm countless hours of work yet still allowed them to bill for it. I no longer use the old computer that was being thrown out by the firm. I have a new custom built machine, high quality color printer and the latest image software available just for this purpose.

Every image I work on, when complete, is burned onto a CD and filed for further reference. To date, I have well over 400 CDs with images that were reworked and presented to clients. Every once in a while someone will come to me and ask. "Do you remember that project we did for XYZ a few years back? Do you have a copy of it?" And I do.

Now that said, we had a draftsperson in the firm who recognized that 3D imaging was coming of age and that it would be an asset to the firm to have that capability. He went to the partners and presented the idea and said that he would like to do it. They said fine they would purchase the program but he had to learn it on his own time. Weeks turned into months. Then one day I asked him how it was coming along. He said, "I am not doing it. If they want it they have to pay me for it." I mentioned that if you show them what you can do, they would be happy to pay you to do the work. He said, "NO" they would have to pay him for his time to learn the program." By the way, this is the same person that was watching a movie on the upper left hand corner on his computer monitor while working on a project during working hours.

You cannot blame them for not wanting to pay you to learn something they did not hire you to do. We are talking about making yourself irreplaceable to the firm. This should not be confused with "on-the-job training" for which you are being trained to do the job you were hired for.

Another draftsperson in our firm took it upon himself to learn how our server backed up files and how to reboot the server when it went off line. He also taught himself some of the little known nuances of the Computer Aided Design program. Now he is our backup person for both and has become our "GO TO" person when problems arise.

These additional skill sets set you apart and make you maybe not irreplaceable but a lot harder to let go and replace.

Another person I know worked at an art gallery in

New York City as a helper. Every once in a while a piece of art needed the frame repaired and he would very carefully make the repair after hours. In a short period of time the gallery would bring in art that needed framing and he became the framer for the gallery. Now he is the art handler for a very prestigious gallery and hangs priceless works of art for its wealthy patrons. All because he took the initiative on his own.

Another Example: A young man, who washed airplanes at a local airport in exchange for an hour of flying lessons, is now a captain for a national airline.

And yet another example: A young woman I know works for an upscale kitchen supplier. She joined an industry association that was noted for its golf outings. She did not play golf and I was wondering how she was going to effectively network the association. She got involved. She sold the

50/50 tickets at the monthly meetings, acted as the greeter to everyone that attended the meetings, she even handled registration for all golf outings. She became so well known that when anyone thought about kitchens, they thought of her. It was a brilliant approach. I may have known 45 percent of the members, she knows them all and they know her by name.

These are just some of the people I know. The list goes on and on. Look around you, examples are everywhere. Although no one is irreplaceable you can make it very hard for a company to let you go.

Look at it this way, the least that can happen is that when you are looking for another job you are worth a lot more then you once were.

Do your job to the very best of your ability, give your employer an honest day's work (that alone will set you apart) and learn something new that you can use to help your company be more competitive and you more valuable. Some may call it brown nosing, I call it being employed.

Chapter Twelve
"All For One. One For All"
The Organization

=====================================

You may be out there looking for new business but in reality it takes the entire organization to make it happen.

=====================================

It is said that it takes an entire village to raise a child. The same is true when it comes to finding, selling and keeping that new account, and for that matter every account.

You may be out there looking for new business but in reality it takes the entire organization to make it happen.

From the person who answers the phone, to the corner office, it is the entire client experience that makes or breaks the relationship you are trying to cultivate. Yes, the entire company. Just like in Chapter V when we were discussing client presentations and the potential client wanted you to make his decision easy. He is also looking for confirmation that he made the right decision every time he contacts your firm.

I remember a story about a company that needed a short term bank loan to finance an expansion of their plant. The principals of the firm went from bank to bank making their presentation. Finally they found a bank that would consider their loan request. The decision-making committee of the bank was split about granting the loan. Reluctantly they agreed to make the loan. The bank president called the company to say that their loan request was approved. The person that answered the phone was extremely rude and he placed the bank president on hold, after being on hold for over 20 minutes he finally hung up. The loan was never offered to the company, the expansion never took place and the principals never knew why.

Now I said the person who answered the phone, not just the receptionist. For it is everybody's responsibility to make anyone who calls your firm feel welcome and to be as helpful as possible. For all the sales and marketing effort in the world cannot make up for poor customer/client service.

For all the sales and marketing effort in the world cannot make up for poor customer/client service.

Another example of poor customer / client service, and this is strictly my opinion, is the automated telephone answering system. You know the one that says for Mr. Miller push 8, Mr. Jones push 3, and so on. I know that there are times when I call a company and do not know who I need to speak to. I may only need a name or just information about their firm. It is as if they are too busy or could not be bothered to answer the phone and assist me in whatever I may need. I guess they assume the caller knows who they want to talk to and they have to go no further.

Here is an example; I heard that this company was looking to purchase a multi-family project. One of our developers was looking to sell a multi-family project that was exactly what this company was looking for. So I called not knowing who it was I should be talking to. I got the recorded message "For Mr. So & So push 2," and so on, but I know the way around this system, so I pushed "O" for operator. The recorded message said "Sorry, invalid entry" or "Please leave your message in the general mail box." Here I am trying to help their company find something they are looking for and the feeling I got was that they did not care. Frustrated, I hung up and called another company, a real live person answered the phone. She directed me to the right person, the lead was passed on and the project was just what they were looking for.

This is not to say that many companies do not make an honest effort, it is just the exception to this rule can not be yours. You have to be one of the best. If you have anything to say about it, do not short cut the customer service process. You can not afford it.

Now sales leads come from almost anywhere. And we discussed several sources earlier in the book. Yet another source, which is often overlooked, is from your co-workers. I get leads from almost everyone in the office. If they drove by a sign about some new development or the name of a developer that they have never heard of, they pull over and copy down the information and give it me.

When they are working with a client they will ask if the client has another project coming up or do they know of someone who has a new project.

I follow up and let them know the outcome of their lead. If it bears fruit I make sure the principals of the firm know where the lead came from and that they get the credit for finding it. They know that nothing happens (no job, no pay check, nothing) until somebody sells something.

It takes the whole team to sell an account and they do it every time they pick up the phone and it can take just one person to lose it.

They know that nothing *happens* (no job, no pay check, nothing) *until somebody sells something.*

Look for the next book. It will be on how to manage your marketing and sales organization, from territorial disputes to the quota systems.

6126228R0

Made in the USA
Lexington, KY
22 July 2010